ITALIAN EQUITY CROWDFUNDING LEGISLATION

LAWS AND REGULATIONS

Alessandro M. Lerro

ISBN-13: 978-1494865719
ISBN-10:1494865718

Copyright © 2014 Alessandro Maria Lerro

Lerro & Partners – Roma – Italy
Via G. Severano, 5, 00161
www.lerro.it
@alessandrolerro

First edition January 2nd, 2014

Printed in the United States of America

All rights reserved. No part of this book may be used or reproduced in any manner whatsoever without prior written consent of the author, except as provided by the United States of America copyright law.

This publication is designed to provide accurate and authoritative information in regard to the subject matter covered. It is sold with the understanding that the publisher and the author are not hereby engaged in rending legal, accounting, or other professional services. If legal advice or other expert assistance is required, the services of competent professional person should be sought.

ITALIAN EQUITY CROWDFUNDING LEGISLATION

CONTENTS

1	About the Author	Pg vii
2	Introduction	Pg 1
3	Framework	Pg 3
4	Consolidated Finance Act	Pg 9
5	CONSOB Regulation	Pg 25
6	Annex 1	Pg 49
7	Annex 2	Pg 53
8	Annex 3	Pg 57

ABOUT THE AUTHOR

ALESSANDRO M. LERRO is an Italian lawyer expert of new technologies and business creation. Founder of LERRO & PARTNERS, he has been advising for years start up and small/medium companies dealing mostly with information technology, healthcare, and media. Alessandro is often involved in merger and acquisition, capital formation, venture capital and investment deals.

He served as board member and C.E.O. in several companies involved in high technology industry and venture capital in Italy, Germany, Luxembourg and U.K..

Author of many articles and of the book "Equity Crowdfunding", published in Italy by Il Sole 24 Ore, Alessandro is a leading lawyer in the crowdfunding and capital formation industry.

Website: www.lerro.it

Blog: www.avvocati.net

Twitter: @alessandrolerro

ALESSANDRO M. LERRO

INTRODUCTION

This book aims to provide foreign readers an English translation of the Italian equity crowdfunding laws and regulations.
It is the first law ever enacted in the world on this subject, so it might be useful for anybody involved in crowdfunding legislation in other countries, as a reference of what Italian legislators and regulators deemed appropriate for this innovative and disruptive financing instrument.

The English version might also be useful for companies interested in understanding how equity crowdfunding works in Italy, and wondering to launch a crowdfunding project from an Italian platform. Indeed, Italy is currently the only Country where equity crowdfunding is fully regulated and a clear and definite set of rules is provided for all the players: regulators, crowdfunding websites, proposed companies, broker-dealers and investors.
Also investors might take advantage of this book, would they be interested to evaluate an investment through an Italian on-line platform.

Nevertheless, this book provides only a free translation of the rules in simple English, as easy as possible; it is not official and it is not to be considered a legal advise. Under Italian law, only the official Italian text is binding and no translation is officially endorsed. Moreover it is highly recommended to ask for the help of an authorized Italian counselor to properly understand the laws and regulations.

ALESSANDRO M. LERRO

FRAMEWORK

In 2012, the Italian Minister of Economic Development set up an expert group (nicknamed "Task Force") to study and propose measures to facilitate economic growth. In September 2012, this team presented a report named "Restart, Italy!", inspired by the best international experience and based on the outcome of extensive public consultations.

In line with the Obama's administration, the Task Force concluded that crowdfunding would allow the participation of a large number of subjects to fund start-ups, through specialized web platforms. The team proposed the establishment of a simple and streamlined authorization process, based on clear guarantees from the operator of the platform; the team also suggested to create transparent information and education tools, to highlight the risks of losing the capital invested, as it indeed happens with most investment.

The work of the Task Force led the Government to take a number of measures both in terms of innovative start-ups and crowdfunding, aiming to "make our country a place where innovation is a factor in sustainable structural growth and in the enhancement of the competitiveness of enterprises" (Explanatory Memorandum to the Growth Decree 2.0).
This was not an upside-down approach but a bottom-up interpretation of a widespread feeling: in a recent survey, Piepoli Institute found that 64% of the Italian people believe that incentives for innovative start-ups help to create jobs for young

people and to fight the current economic crisis. Indeed, the whole country is benefiting from the development of an innovation-oriented business system, both in terms of domestic gross product and employment.

The legal basis of crowdfunding Italian laws is the Law Decree dated October 18, 2012 n. 179 ("Further urgent measure for the growth of the country" currently referred to as "Growth Decree 2.0"), which was finally approved with amendments by the Law dated December 17, 2012 n. 221.
An entire section of such Decree contains "Measures for the creation and development of start-up companies" (Articles 25 to 32). Further modifications were introduced by Article 9, paragraph 16, of the Law Decree dated June 28, 2013 n. 76.
These rules identify innovative start-ups, which at the moment are the only companies suitable to be funded by the crowd through online platforms. The Decree also recognizes the role of company incubators, having they showed, in the last decade, to be valuable to encourage the creation and growth of start-ups.

While in the USA the JOBS Act has dedicated equity crowdfunding to the EGC (Emerging Growth Company), granting eligibility to a very wide set of enterprises despite their area of business, Italy has allowed equity crowdfunding only to innovative start-ups, duly identified on the basis of a set of features and requirements. Indeed, Italian crowdfunding law was issued within a specific start-ups regulation, so it was quite an obvious choice. There is ground to guess that it will be extended to other compatible areas, since there is no particular reason to exclude them.

The Growth Decree 2.0 implicitly but quite clearly states that the rules laid down do regulate equity-based crowdfunding, and no other crowdfunding models, already sufficiently regulated and characterized by a lower hazard for the consumer.

Indeed, donation-based crowdfunding doesn't leave much room for deception, as it is not about investment but gift. The user is not likely to lose anything because he doesn't expect to get anything in return: it is just an act of generosity. Obviously there is the risk of being misled about the destination of the donation, but such deception can exist in any proposed charity, regardless the fund raising instrument (web platform).

Even in reward-based crowdfunding consumer's interest is poorly exposed to risks, given that the reward offered against financing is generally small and not suitable of economic assessment: far from being considered a consideration, it is generally a mere acknowledgment, sometimes a gadget, sometimes a moral recognition or its realization (i.e. a loyalty card or a status of VIP).

Donation and reward-based crowdfunding are very similar to each other under this point of view. Italian law provides the donor with a specific right of termination in the event of default by the beneficiary of the grant (art. 793 Civil Code).

The other two formulas of reward-based crowdfunding, the pre-order and profit sharing are sufficiently regulated as well, although possible overlaps between profit sharing and equity crowdfunding should be assessed.

Quite different is the lending-based model. Also in this case Italian law provides the lender with appropriate guarantees while platforms business is overseen and monitored by the Bank of Italy, as every other lending business. Moreover, the level of attention generally dedicated to lending money to a third party is very different from that you might expect for a financial investment: moneylenders know that it will not be easy or obvious to have their money back and usually take appropriate precautions.

Therefore, it is clear that the non-inclusion of the other three crowdfunding models does not mean any ban, being they either free or already regulated or otherwise not subject to further limitations.

U.S. crowdfunding law was dedicated to small businesses for which it considered a collection limit of a million dollars a year fair enough. Italian law, instead, aimed at raising equity for innovative start-ups, and set a much higher limit at 5 million euros (approximately $ 6.7 millions) per year. This approach is consistent with the target, since one million dollars can't bring innovation far enough. The Italian choice also makes sense considering the poor diffusion of business angel and venture capital in the Country, reduced even further after 2008. So the American practice to perform multiple rounds of financing to the progress of the business project works in the U.S. and similar countries, whose capital market is mature. It would not work well in Italy, where the same maturity and elasticity miss, with the result that a company well established and adequately seeded, might suddenly find itself without resources and unable to find more on the capital market. Moreover, the recapitalization process of an innovative company might be very expensive, as the company needs to communicate science and not the sale of hamburger or the production of beautiful floral creations. If this type of communication must be periodically reactivated, it is likely to absorb most of the finances collected.

Italian equity crowdfunding law is based on only four articles that article 30 of the Growth Decree 2.0 has added to Legislative Decree dated February 24, 1998 no. 58, better known as CFA (Consolidated Finance Act, or in Italian: TUF, Testo Unico della Finanza):
a) Article 1, paragraph 5 novies and decies, CFA, which define capital-raising web platforms;
b) Article 50 quinquies CFA, about the management of web platforms;
c) Article 100 ter CFA, about offers of equity subscription through online platforms;
d) Article 190, paragraph 1, CFA, relating to penalties for intermediaries, which now also includes the online platforms.

Therefore, equity crowdfunding law has been inserted in the picture of finance laws, which is quite a wide set of rules, including:
1) the Consolidated Law on Finance (CFA);
2) CONSOB Regulation dated October 29, 2007 n. 16190 (so called Intermediaries Regulation);
3) CONSOB and Bank of Italy Regulation dated October 29, 2007 (so called Joint Regulation).

As the JOBS Act has delegated to the S.E.C. (Securities and Exchange Commission) the development and the adoption of a regulation implementing crowdfunding law, so the Italian law has delegated the CONSOB, which is the Italian supervisory authority, to enact the law.

The legal powers of CONSOB regulations in the subject matter are twofold. According to the new art. 50 quinquies, CFA,

CONSOB :
a) decide the integrity requirements for entities that have control of an on-line platform and for individuals running administration, management and control;
b) determine, by regulation, principles and criteria relating to:
1. the formation of the register and any related form of advertising;
2. any additional condition for the entry in the register, the grounds for suspension, cancellation and readmission;
3. any additional ground of incompatibility;
4. the rules of conduct that operators must comply with in the relationship with investors, providing a simplified regime for professional clients.

In addition, on the basis of the new art. 100 ter, CFA, CONSOB defines the rules applicable to tenders proposed through on-line platforms, in order:
a) to reserve professional investors or special categories of investors a share of the securities being offered, when the offer is not restricted exclusively to professional investors;
b) to protect non-professional investors in the event that the controlling shareholders of innovative start-ups transfer their shares to a third party after the offer.

Following the legislative delegation, CONSOB opened the regulatory process, produced a Regulatory Impact Analysis in order to assess any available options and to identify the more efficient, transparent and less costly solutions. After a pre-consultation with qualified stakeholders, CONSOB opened a consultation in crowdsourcing on a draft regulation.

Finally, the "Regulations about the collection of equity for innovative start-ups through web platforms" (in short Crowdfunding Regulation) was adopted with CONSOB Resolution no. 18592 dated June 26, 2013.

The translations hereinafter provided include the equity crowdfunding rules added to the CFA (equity crowdfunding laws) and the whole CONSOB Regulation with its annexes (equity crowdfunding regulations).

ALESSANDRO M. LERRO

CONSOLIDATED FINANCE ACT

(Testo Unico della Finanza)

Legislative Decree February 24, 1998, n. 58

Selection of Rules

Introduced by the Growth Decree 2.0

(Law Decree 18.10.2012 n. 179)

Article 1

(Definitions)

1. In this legislative decree:

a) "Bankruptcy Law" shall mean Royal Decree no. 267 of 16 March 1942 and subsequent amendments;

b) "Consolidated Banking Law" shall mean Legislative Decree no. 385 of 1 September 1993 and subsequent amendments;

c) "CONSOB" shall mean National Commission for the companies and the stock exchange;

d) "Isvap" shall mean Institute for monitoring of private and public interest insurance companies;

d-bis) "ESFS": the European System of Financial Supervision comprising the following parts:

    1) "EBA": European Banking Authority, established by Regulation (EU) No 1093/2010;

    2) "EIOPA": European Insurance and Occupational Pensions Authority, established by Regulation (EU) No 1094/2010;

    3) "ESMA": European Securities and Markets Authority, established by Regulation (EU) No 1095/2010;

    4) "Joint Committee": the Joint Committee of the European supervisory authorities, envisaged by article 54 of Regulation (EU) No. 1093/2010, of Regulation (EU) No. 1094/2010, of Regulation (EU) No. 1095/2010;

    5) "ESRB": European Systemic Risk Board, established by Regulation (EU) No 1092/2010;

    6) "Member State supervisory authorities": the competent authorities or supervisory authorities of Member States specified in the deeds of the Union pursuant to article 1, section 2 of Regulation (EU) No 1093/2010, of Regulation (EU) No 1094/2010 and of Regulation (EU) No 1095/2010;

e) "Italian investment company" shall mean an undertaking, other than a bank or a financial intermediary entered in the register referred to in Article 107 of the Consolidated Law on Banking, authorized to provide investment services or activities having its registered office and head office in Italy;

f) "EU investment company" shall mean an undertaking, other than a bank, authorized to provide investment services or activities having its registered office and head office in the same member state of the European Union, other than Italy;

g) "non-EU investment company" shall mean an undertaking, other than a bank, authorized to provide investment services or activities, having its registered office in a state that is not a member of the European Union;

h) "investment companies" shall mean any Italian, EU and non-EU investment company;

i) "Società di investimento a capitale variabile" (SICAV) shall mean an open-end investment company having its registered office and head office in Italy and the exclusive purpose of collective investment of the capital raised by offering its shares to the public;

j) "investment fund": shall mean the fund raised independently against the issue of one or more stakes from a number of investors, with the aim of investing the money raised according to a pre-established investment policy; it is divided into units pertaining to a given number of investors and it is fully independently managed in the interests of the investors;

k) "open-end fund" shall mean a mutual fund whose participants have the right to request, at any time, to redeem stakes in accordance with the procedures established by the rules of the fund;

l) "closed-end fund" shall mean a mutual fund in which the right to redeem stakes may be exercised by participants only at predetermined steps;

m) "collective investment undertakings" shall mean mutual funds and SICAVs;

m-bis) "Harmonized UCITS": UCITS falling under the scope of application of Directive 2009/65/EC and related enactment provisions;

m-ter) "EU UCITS": UCITS established in an EU Member State other than Italy;

m-quater) "Non-EU UCITS": UCITS established in a non-EU Member State;

m-quinquies) "Feeder UCITS": the UCITS that invests its assets entirely or mainly in the master UCITS;

m-sexies) "Master UCITS": the UCITS in which one or more feeder UCITS invest all or most of their assets;

n) "collective portfolio management" shall mean the service that is performed through:

> 1) the promotion, establishment and organization of mutual funds and the administration of participants' accounts;
>
> 2) the management of the assets of own or third-party collective investment undertakings by means of investment in financial instruments, claims and other movable or immovable assets;
>
> 2-bis) marketing of units or shares of own UCITS;

o) "asset management company" shall mean a company having its registered office and head office in Italy authorized to provide the service of collective portfolio management;

o-bis) "harmonized asset management company" shall mean a company having its registered office and head office in an EU country other than Italy authorized under the UCITS Directive to provide the service of collective portfolio management;

p) "promoter" shall mean an Italian asset management company that performs the activity indicated in paragraph n), point 1);

q) "manager" shall mean an Italian asset management company that performs the activity indicated in paragraph n), point 2);

q-bis) "manager of the master UCITS": the management company managing the master UCITS or master SICAV;

q-ter) "manager of the feeder UCITS": the management company managing the feeder UCITS or feeder SICAV;

q-quater) "depositary of the master UCITS or feeder UCITS": the deposit bank of the master UCITS or feeder UCITS or, if the master UCITS or feeder UCITS are EU or non-EU UCITS, the subject in the country of origin authorized to carry out the duties of deposit bank;

r) "authorized intermediaries" shall mean investment companies (SIM), EU investment companies with branches in Italy, non-EU investment companies, asset management companies, harmonized asset management companies with branch in Italy, SICAVs and financial intermediaries entered in the register referred to in Article 107 of the Consolidated Banking Law and Italian banks, EU banks with branches in Italy and non-EU banks, authorized to engage in investment services or activities;

r-bis) "Home Member State of the harmonized management company": the EU Member State where the harmonized management company has its registered office and general management;

r-ter) "Home Member State of the UCITS": EU Member State in which the UCITS was established;

s) "services subject to mutual recognition" shall mean the activities and services listed in sections A and B of the table annexed to this decree, authorized in the home EU member state;

t) "public offering or investment incentive" shall mean every offer or incentive, invitation to offer or promotional message, in whatsoever form addressed to the public, whose objective is the sale or subscription of financial products including the allocation through authorized people;

u) "financial products" shall mean financial instruments and every other form of investment of a financial nature; bank or postal deposits without the issue of financial instruments shall not constitute financial products;

v) "public offer to buy or exchange" shall mean every offer, invitation to offer or promotional message, in whatsoever form effected, whose objective is the purchase or exchange of financial products, addressed to a number of persons and of a total amount greater than that indicated in the regulation pursuant to article 100, subsection 1, paragraphs b) and c); an offering of securities issued by the central banks of EU Member States shall not constitute a mandatory takeover bid or exchange tender offering;

w) "listed issuers" shall mean Italian or foreign issuers of financial instruments listed on Italian regulated markets;

w-bis) "financial products issued by insurance companies": the policies and operations referred to in the sectors on Life III and V according to Article 2, Subsection 1, of the Legislative Decree No. 209 of September 7, 2005, with the exclusion of individual pension schemes according to Article 13, Subsection 1, paragraph b), of Legislative Decree No. 252 of September 5, 2005;

w-ter) "regulated market": shall mean a multilateral system which permits or facilitates the meeting, internally and according to non-discretional regulations, of multiple third party purchase and sale interests with regard to financial instruments, admitted to trading in compliance with the rules of the market, in order to effect contracts, and which is operated by a management company, is authorized and operates regularly;

w-quater) "listed issuers with Italy as home member state":

1) issuers with shares admitted to trading on Italian regulated markets or of another EU Member State, having their registered office in Italy;

2) issuers of debt securities with a nominal unit value of less than one thousand Euro, or corresponding value in a different currency, admitted to trading on Italian regulated markets or those of another EU Member State, with registered office in Italy;

3) issuers of securities indicated under points 1) and 2), with registered office in a non-EU country, for which the first application for admission to trading on an EU regulated market was submitted in Italy or Italy was later chosen as the home member state when said first application for admission was not implemented by decision of the issuer;

4) issuers of securities other than those indicated under points 1) and 2), with registered office in Italy or whose securities are admitted to trading on an Italian regulated market and who have adopted Italy as the home Member State. The issuer may choose one Member State only as the home member state. The decision shall remain valid for at least three years, unless the issuer's securities are no longer admitted to trading on any EU regulated market.

w-quinquies) "central counterparties": the subjects indicated in article 2, point 1), of Regulation (EU) no. 648/2012 of the European Parliament and of the Council, of 4 July 2012, concerning OTC derivative instruments, central counterparties and the recorded data on the transactions.

1-bis. "Securities" shall mean categories of securities for trading on the capital market, such as:

a) company shares and other shares equivalent to

shares of companies, partnerships or other persons and share deposit certificates;

b) bonds and other debt securities, including certificates of deposit relating to such securities;

c) any other security normally negotiated which permits the purchase or sale of securities indicated in the preceding paragraphs;

d) any other security usually involving cash settlement determined with reference to securities indicated in the preceding paragraphs, to currency, interest rates, returns, commodities, indices or measures.

1-ter. "Money market instruments" shall mean categories of instruments normally negotiated on the money market, such as Treasury bonds, certificates of deposit and commercial bills.

2. "Financial instruments" shall mean:

a) securities;

b) money market instruments;

c) units in collective investment undertakings;

d) options, futures, swaps, futures contracts on interest rates and other derivative contracts linked to securities, currency, interest rates or returns, or other derivatives, financial indices or measures that may be settled by the physical delivery of the underlying asset or by cash payment of differentials;

e) options, futures, swaps, interest rate swaps, and any other derivative contracts on commodities, settlement of which is by payment of the differentials in cash, or at the discretion of one of the parties, except in cases where such option is the result of default or other event leading to cancellation of the contract;

f) options, futures, swaps and other derivative contracts on commodities, the settlement of which may be by physical delivery of the underlying asset and which are traded on a regulated market and/or multilateral trading systems;

g) options, futures, swaps, forward contracts and other derivative contracts on commodities, the settlement of which may be by physical delivery of the underlying asset, other than those indicated in paragraph f), that have no commercial purpose, and with the characteristics of other derivatives, taking into consideration, amongst other things, whether they are cleared and executed through recognized clearing houses or whether they are subject to regular margin calls;

h) derivatives for the transfer of credit risk;

i) differential financial contracts;

j) options, futures, swaps, futures contracts, swaps, futures contracts on interest rates and other derivative contracts related to climatic variables, transport rates, emission levels, inflation rates or other official economic statistics, settled by cash payment of differentials or at the discretion of one of the parties, except in cases where such option is the result of default or other event leading to cancellation of the contract and other derivative contracts on assets, options, bonds, indices and measures other than those indicated in previous paragraphs, with the characteristics of other derivative financial instruments, taking into consideration, amongst other things, whether are traded on a regulated market or multilateral trading systems, whether they are cleared and executed through a recognized clearing house or whether they are subject to regular margin calls.

2-bis. The Minister of the Economy and Finance, by the regulation pursuant to Article 18, subsection 5, shall identify:

a) the other derivative contracts pursuant to subsection 2, paragraph g), with the characteristics of other derivatives, cleared and executed through recognized clearing houses or subject to regular margin calls;

b) the other derivative contracts pursuant to subsection 2, paragraph j), with the characteristics of other derivatives, traded on a regular market or through multilateral trading systems, cleared and executed through recognized clearing houses or subject to regular margin calls;

3. "Derivatives" shall mean the financial instruments specified in subsection 2, paragraphs d), e), f), g), h), i) and j), as well as the financial instruments specified in subsection 1-bis, paragraph d).

4. The payment instruments are not financial instruments. Financial instruments, and specifically swaps, are foreign currency buy and sell contracts, extraneous to commercial transactions and settled on the difference, also by means of automatic "roll-over" transactions. The additional foreign currency transactions identified pursuant to article 18, subsection 5, are also financial instruments.

5. "Investment services and activities" shall mean the following activities where they concern financial instruments:

a) dealing for own account;

b) execution of orders for clients;

c) subscription and/or placement with firm commitment underwriting or standby commitments to issuers;

c-bis) placement without firm or standby commitment to issuers;

d) portfolio management;

e) reception and transmission of orders;

f) investment consultancy,

g) management of multilateral trading systems.

5-bis. " Trading on own account" shall mean buy and sell transactions of financial instruments, directly and in relation to customer orders, together with market maker activities.

5-ter. " Systematic internalizer" shall mean the person who, in an organized, frequent and systematic manner, trades on his own account executing customer orders outside a regulated market or multilateral trading systems.

5-quarter. " Market maker" shall mean a person offering his services to trade directly on regulated markets and multilateral trading systems on a continuous basis, buying and selling financial instruments at self-established prices.

5-quinquies. " Portfolio management" shall mean the management, on a discretionary and individual basis, of portfolio investments, which include one or more financial instruments and according to mandate conferred by customers.

5-sexies. The service pursuant to subsection 5, paragraph e), including the receipt and transmission of orders as well as consistent activities to place two or more investors in contact, thereby making it possible to conclude transactions by mediation.

5-septies. "Investment consultancy" shall mean the provision of customized recommendations to a customer upon request or as an initiative by the service provider, regarding one or more transaction on an identified financial instrument. The recommendation shall be customized when it is presented as suitable for the customer or is based on consideration of the customer's characteristics. A recommendation shall not be customized if disclosed to the public through distribution channels.

5-octies. "Multilateral trading systems management"

shall mean the management of multilateral trading systems which permit the meeting, within and on the basis of non-discretional rules, of multiple third party purchase and sale interests relating to financial instruments, in such a way as to give rise to contracts.

5-novies. A "web platform for the collection of capital for innovative start-ups" is an on-line platform whose exclusive purpose is to facilitate the collection of equity for innovative start-ups, including start-ups with social purposes.

5-decies. An "innovative start-up" is a company as defined by article 25, paragraph 2, of the Law Decree October 18, 2012, no. 179.

6. "Non-core services" shall mean the following:

a) safekeeping and administration of financial instruments and related services;

b) safe custody services;

c) lending to investors to enable them to carry out transactions in financial instruments where the lender is involved in the transaction;

d) advice to undertakings on capital structure, industrial strategy and related matters and advice and services relating to mergers and the purchase of undertakings;

e) services related to the issue or placement of financial instruments, including the organization and constitution of underwriting and placement syndicates;

f) Investment research and financial analysis or other forms of general recommendation regarding transactions on financial instruments;

g) foreign exchange trading where this is connected with the provision of investment services.

g-bis) activities and services identified by regulation by the Minister of the Economy and Finance, after consulting the Bank of Italy and CONSOB, and relating to the provision of investment or accessory services on derivatives.

6-bis. "Shareholdings or holdings" shall mean shares, capital parts and other financial instruments that confer administrative rights or in any case those provided for by the final subsection of Article 2351 of the Civil Code.

6-ter. Except as specified, the provisions of this legislative decree that refer to the board of directors, the administrative body or the directors shall also apply to the management board and the members thereof.

6-quater. Except as specified, the provisions of this legislative decree that refer to the board of auditors, the members thereof or the control body shall also apply to the supervisory board, the management control committee and the members thereof.

Article 50-quinquies

(Management of web platform for the collection of capital for innovative start-ups)

1. A web platform manager is the subject, which professionally manages the web platform for the collection of equity for innovative start-ups, and which is entered in the register referred to in paragraph 2.

2. The management of web platforms for the collection of equity for innovative start-ups is reserved either to investment companies and banks authorized to provide investment services and to the subjects entered in a special register managed by CONSOB, provided that the latter transmit any equity subscription and trading order exclusively to banks and investment companies. The subjects registered in the said register are not subject to the provisions of Part II, Title II, Chapter II and of article 32.

3. The entry in the register referred to in paragraph 2 is subject to the following requisites:

a) the enterprise must be a company limited by shares, a limited partnership with a share capital, a limited liability company or a cooperative company;

b) its registered and administrative office or, for EU subjects, its permanent establishment, must be located in Italy;

c) the company's purpose must be compliant to what stated in paragraph 1;

d) the controlling shareholders and the executives in charge with administration, direction and control must meet the reputation requirements established by CONSOB;

e) the executives in charge with administration, direction and control must meet the professionalism requirements established by CONSOB;

4. The subjects entered in the register referred to in paragraph 2 may not hold money or financial instruments belonging to third parties.

5. CONSOB determines, by regulation, the principles and criteria relative to:

a) the register formation and its publicity;

b) any other conditions for the entry in the register, reasons for suspension, for cancellation and for readmission, and any measures applicable to the registered subjects;

c) any other incompatibility causes;

d) the rules of conduct that web platforms managers must respect in their relations with investors, providing simplified rules for professional customers.

6. CONSOB monitors web platforms managers to

check on compliance with the rules of this article and any implementation rules thereafter. At this purpose, CONSOB may request the communication of data and information, the transmission of deeds and documents, stating the relative terms, and may also carry out inspections.

7. Web platforms managers who breach the rules of this article or any implementation rule issued by CONSOB thereafter, are punished with a fine from five hundred euro to twenty five thousand euro, based on the severity of the breach and any eventual recidivism. Any subject in the register referred to in paragraph 2 may also be suspended from one to four months or cancelled from the register. Paragraphs 2 and 3 of article 196 are applied. The provisions of Part II, Title IV, Chapter I, remain binding for investment companies, banks, asset management companies and harmonized management companies.

Article 100-ter

(Offers through platforms for the collection of equity)

1. Public offers conducted exclusively through one or more web platforms for the collection of equity may have the sole purpose of the subscribing of financial instruments issued by innovative start-ups and may not exceed the amount determined by CONSOB pursuant to article 100, subsection 1, letter c).

2. CONSOB states the rules for the offers referred to in the preceding paragraph, in order to ensure that, whenever the offer is not reserved exclusively to professional customers, a part of the financial instruments offered are subscribed by professional investors or special categories of investors identified by CONSOB, and to protect retail investors if the controlling shareholders of the innovative start-up transfer their own shares to third parties after the offer.

Article 190

(Other financial penalties regarding intermediaries, markets and the central depository system for financial instruments)

1. Subjects carrying out administrative or managerial tasks and employees of companies or qualified entities, which do not comply with the provisions established by Articles 6; 7, paragraphs 2 and 3; 8, paragraph 1; 9; 10; 12; 13, paragraph 2; 21; 22; 24, paragraph 1; 25; 25-bis, paragraphs 1 and 2; 27, paragraphs 3 and 4; 28, paragraph 3; 30, paragraphs 3, 4 and 5; 31, paragraphs 1, 2, 5, 6 and 7; 32, paragraph 2; 33, paragraph 4; 36, paragraphs 2, 3, 4, 6 and 7; 37; 38, paragraphs 3 and 4; 39, paragraphs 1 and 2; 40, paragraph 1; 41, paragraphs 2 and 3; 41-bis ; 42, paragraphs 1, 3, 4, 6, 7 and 8; 43, paragraphs 7 and 8; 50; 50-bis , paragraphs 2, 4 and 5, 50-ter, paragraph 4; 50-quater, paragraph 4; 65; 79-bis; 187-nonies , or the general or special provisions issued by the Bank of Italy or CONSOB on the basis of these same articles, are punished by an administrative fine of two thousand five hundred euro to two hundred and fifty thousand euro. The same fine also applies in the event of breach of Article 18, paragraphs 1 or in case of practice of financial consulting, financial promotion or web platforms management without entry in the registers provided by articles 18-bis, 31 and 50-quinquies.

2. ...omissis...

CONSOB REGULATION

"Collection of equity by innovative start-ups through web platforms"

CONTENTS

PART I – GENERAL PROVISIONS

Art. 1 – *Legal basis*

Art. 2 - *Definitions*

Art. 3 - *Procedures for communication and transmission to CONSOB*

PART II - REGISTER AND RULES FOR WEB PLATFORMS

Title I – Establishment of the Register

Art. 4 – *Establishment of the register*

Art. 5 – *Contents of the register*

Art. 6 – *Publicity of the register*

Title II – Registration

Art. 7 - *Registration procedure*

Art. 8 – *Reputation requirements for the controlling*

shareholders

Art. 9 – *Reputation and professionalism requirements for administrators, directors and controllers*

Art. 10 - *Effects of the loss of the reputation requirements*

Art. 11 - *Suspension of administrators, directors and controllers from the office*

Art. 12 - *Cancellation from the register*

Title III - Rules of conduct

Art. 13 – *Web platform manager's obligations*

Art. 14 - *Information about the web platform management*

Art. 15 - *Information about the investment in innovative start-ups*

Art. 16 - *Information about the offers*

Art. 17 - *Obligations relating to the processing of investment orders*

Art. 18 - *Obligations relating to investors protection from operational risks*

Art. 19 - *Confidentiality obligations*

Art. 20 – *Record keeping obligations*

Art. 21 – *Disclosure to CONSOB*

Title IV - Sanctions and precautionary measures

Art. 22 - *Precautionary measures*

Art. 23 - *Sanctions*

PART III - RULES ABOUT OFFERS THROUGH WEB

PLATFORMS

Art. 24 – *Terms concerning the offers on the web platforms*

Art. 25 – *Funding and right of revocation*

Annex 1 - Instructions for filing an application to the web platforms register and for the annotation in the special section

Annex 2 - Report on the company's business and organizational structure

Annex 3 - Information about the offer

ALESSANDRO M. LERRO

PART I

GENERAL PROVISIONS

Art. 1

(*Legal basis*)

1. This regulation is adopted pursuant to articles 50-*quinquies* and 100-*ter* of Legislative Decree dated February 24, 1998, no. 58.

Art. 2

(*Definitions*)

1. For the purposes of this Regulation:

a) "Consolidated Finance Act" shall mean Legislative Decree dated February 24, 1998, no. 58;
b) «decree» shall mean Law Decree dated 18 October 18, 2012, no. 179 converted into law with amendments by Law dated December 17, 2012 no. 221 introducing "Further urgent measures for the growth of the Country";
c) «issuer» shall mean the innovative start-up company, including start-ups having social purposes, as defined by article 25, paragraphs 2 and 4, of the decree;
d) «web platform» shall mean the on-line platform with the exclusive purpose of facilitating the collection of equity by innovative start-ups;
e) «manager» shall mean the subject which professionally operates the equity crowdfunding web for innovative start-ups, entered on the specific register kept by the CONSOB;
f) «control» shall mean the case in which, directly or indirectly an individual, a legal entity or several persons jointly, also by means of shareholders'

agreements, holds either the majority of the votes in the ordinary shareholders' meeting, or sufficient enough to exercise a dominating influence on the ordinary shareholders' meeting;

g) «offer» shall mean the offer to the public carried out exclusively via one or more equity crowdfunding web platform, concerning securities issued by innovative start-ups for a total consideration below the maximum amount stated by CONSOB pursuant to article 34-*ter*, paragraph 1, letter *c)* of the CONSOB regulation about issuers, adopted by the resolution dated May 14, 1999 no. 11971 and any modification thereafter;

h) «financial instruments» shall mean the shares or shareholdings representing the share capital, as provided for by the decree, issued by innovative start-ups, being offered to the crowd through the web platforms;

i) «register» shall mean the register held by the CONSOB pursuant to article 50-*quinquies* of the Consolidated Finance Act;

j) «professional investors» shall mean the private professional clients as identified by Annex 3, par. I, of the CONSOB Regulation about intermediaries, adopted with resolution dated October 29, 2007, no. 16190 and any modification thereafter, and the public professional clients as defined by article 2 of the Ministry of Economy and Finance dated November 11, 2011 no. 236.

Art. 3

(*Procedures for communication and transmission to CONSOB*)

1. Each application, communication, deed, document and any other information required by this regulation are transmitted by certified e-mail (PEC) to portalicrowdfunding@pec.CONSOB.it.

PART II

REGISTER AND RULES FOR WEB PLATFORMS

Title I

Establishment of the register

Art. 4

(Establishment of the register)

1. The register of the web platforms managers is hereby established pursuant to article 50-*quinquies*, paragraph 2, of the Consolidated Law.

2. A special section is annexed to the register, recording investment companies and banks authorized to provide investment services which, before starting operations, must notify CONSOB that they manage a web platform as contemplated by Appendix 1.

Art. 5

(Content of the register)

1. For each registered equity crowdfunding web platform, the following information shall be provided:

a) registration number;
b) company name;
c) Internet URL of the web platform and any corresponding hyperlink;
d) the registered office and the head office address;
e) the permanent establishment in the Italy for EU entities;
f) details of any sanctions and precautionary provisions adopted by the CONSOB.

2. The special section of the register provides:

a) company name;
b) Internet URL of the web platform and any corresponding hyperlink;
c) details of any sanctions and precautionary provisions adopted by CONSOB.

Art. 6

(Publicity of the register)

1. The register is published in the "Registers and Lists" section of the electronic CONSOB Bulletin.

Title II

Registration

Art. 7

(Registration procedure)

1. The application for registration is prepared pursuant to the provisions set forth by Annex 1 and it must be accompanied by a report on the company's business and organizational structure, including description of any eventual outsourcing of key operational functions, drafted pursuant to Annex 2.

2. Within seven days of receipt, CONSOB shall verify the regularity and the completeness of the application and shall give the applicant notice of any missing documentation, which shall be sent to CONSOB within thirty days of receipt of the notification.

3. During the investigation, CONSOB may request additional information to:

      a) the applicant company;
      b) individuals that run administrative, direction and control duties for the applicant company;

c) those who control of the applicant company.

In such a case, the investigations deadline shall be suspended from the date of the information request until the date of the information receipt.

4. In the course of the investigation, any change in the requirements for the entry in the register is communicated to CONSOB without delay. Within seven days of the event, the applicant shall submit CONSOB any material documentation thereof. The investigations deadline shall remain suspended from the date of receipt by CONSOB of the communication of changes until the date of receipt of the proper documentation.

5. CONSOB decides the application within sixty days. Registration is denied would the applicant lack the requirements set forth by article 5-*quinquies* of the Consolidated Finance Act and by articles 8 and 9 of this Regulation, or when the applicant's capacity to correctly manage an equity crowdfunding web platform is not the assessed by the contents of the report referred to by Annex 2.

Art. 8

(Reputation requirements for the controlling shareholders)

1. For the purpose of obtaining and keeping registration, the controlling shareholders of the applicant company must declare, under their own responsibility and according to the terms and conditions indicated in Annex 1, that:

a) they have not been interdicted, under supervision or sentenced to punishment involving public duties interdiction, even temporary, and that they have the capacity to run directors' duties;
b) they are not under precautionary measures imposed by the judicial authority under Legislative Decree

dated September 6, 2011 no. 159, and any modification thereafter, without prejudice to the effects of rehabilitation;

c) unless rehabilitated, they have not been sentenced in a non-appealable judgment to:
   1) imprisonment for a crime under the rules governing banking, finance, securities and insurance activities or under the rules on securities markets, securities or payment instruments;
   2) imprisonment for one of the crimes provided for by title XI of book V of the Civil Code and by Royal Decree dated March 16, 1942, no. 267;
   3) imprisonment for a term of not less than one year for a crime against public administration, public trust, property, public order or public economy or for a tax crime;
   4) imprisonment for a term of not less than two years for any intentional crime;

d) that they have not been sentenced to one of the punishments referred to in letter c) with a judgment which applies the punishment at the request of the parties, unless the crime has been extinguished.

2. If control is held by one or more corporate entities, the reputation requirements set forth in paragraph 1 shall be referred to their directors and general manager, or to the individuals running equivalent duties, and to the individuals who control such corporate entities.

Art. 9

(Reputation and professionalism requirements for administrators, directors and controllers)

1. For the purpose of registration and to remain in the register, those who run administration, direction and control of the company must meet the reputation requirements set forth by article 8, paragraph 1.

2. The individuals referred to in paragraph 1 shall be chosen according to professional standing and competence among people who have gained proven track record of two years at least in:

a) acting as administrators, directors or controllers of companies;
b) performing professional activities related to credit, financial securities or insurance;
c) university teaching in legal or economic subjects;
d) administrative or managerial functions in public or private entities or public bodies involved with credit, finance, securities or insurance; or in public entities or public bodies outside such sectors, provided that their duties involved the management of economic-financial resources.

3. Individuals which have gained proven work experience of at least two years in high innovative industry, information technology or technical-scientific areas, or which have been teaching or researching in such areas, can be appointed as non executive members of the board of directors, provided that the majority of the board meets the requirements set fort in paragraph 2.

4. Administrators, directors and controllers for a registered equity crowdfunding platform may not run equivalent positions for other companies which carry out the same activity, unless they belong to the same group.

Art. 10

(Effects of the loss of the reputation requirements)

1. The controlling shareholders and administrators, directors and controllers of an equity crowdfunding web platform shall immediately refer any loss of the reputation requirements to their management and supervisory bodies.

2. In case of loss of the reputation requirements indicated under paragraph 1, the equity crowdfunding web platform shall be cancelled from the register, unless said requirements are restored within a maximum term of two months.

3. During the term set forth under paragraph 2, the equity crowdfunding web platform cannot publish new offers; unless the prescribed requirements are restored, any current offers shall be suspended as of the communication required pursuant to paragraph 1 and shall lapse on the expiry of the two month term.

Art. 11

(Suspension of administrators, directors and controllers from the office)

1. Administrators, directors and controllers of an equity crowdfunding web platform will be suspended if:

a) they are condemned by non final judgment for one of the crimes provided by article 8, paragraph 1, letter c);

b) they are condemned by non final judgment at request of the parties to one of the penalties indicated by article 8, paragraph 1, letter c);

c) they are subject to provisional application of one of the measures provided by articles 67 and 76, paragraph 8, of Legislative Decree dated September 6, 2011 no. 159;

d) they are submitted to a personal precautionary measure.

2. The directors must declare the suspension by a specific resolution within thirty days from the knowledge of the events contemplated under paragraph 1 and must include the revocation in the agenda of the next shareholders' meeting. In the cases provided by letters

c) and d) of paragraph 1, the suspension will last for the entire duration of the measures.

Art. 12

(*Cancellation from the register*)

1. The CONSOB shall cancel a web platform from the register in the following cases:

a) web platform manager's request;

b) loss of the registration requirements;

c) failure to pay the supervisory contributions annually determined by CONSOB;

d) adoption of a cancellation decision pursuant to article 23, paragraph 1, letter b).

2. Web platforms cancelled from the register pursuant to paragraph 1 may be re-entered in the register provided that:

a) they meet again the requirements referred to in articles 8 and 9, in cases referred to in paragraph 1, letters b) and c), or they have paid any supervisory contribution due;

b) three years have elapsed since the date of the notification of cancellation, in cases pursuant to paragraph 1, letter d).

Title III

Rules of conduct

Art. 13

(*The web platform manager's obligations*)

1. The web platform shall operate with diligence, fairness and transparency, avoiding any conflicts of interest which could arise in the management of the web platform that may affect the interests of the investors and the issuers, and ensuring equal treatment to the investors.

2. The web platform shall make available to the investors all the information provided by the issuer about the offer, in a detailed, correct, not misleading manner and without omissions, so that the investors can reasonably and completely understand the nature of the investment, the kind of financial instrument offered and the risks involved, so to take aware investment decisions.

3. The web platform shall draw non-professional investors' attention to the fact that high risky financial investments should be adequately proportionate to their financial resources. The web platform shall not circulate news that is not consistent with the information published on the website and shall refrain from recommending financial instruments and influence the subscription trend.

4. The web platform ensures that the information provided by the website is updated, accessible for 12 months at least after the offers closing and made available upon request for a period of five years from the date of closing.

5. The web platform must grant non-professional investors a withdrawal right from the subscription, free of any charge, to be communicated to the platform within seven days from the order.

Art. 14

(Information about the web platform management)

1. The web platform must contain, in a summarized and

easily comprehensible form, also by means of multimedia techniques, the information regarding:

a. the web platform, its controlling shareholders, its administrators, directors and controllers;
b. the activities performed, including the methods for selecting the offers, and any eventual operations outsourced to third parties;
c. the procedures for orders management as far as the financial instruments offered are concerned, also with reference to the conditions provided by article 17, paragraph 4;
d. any costs charged to investors;
e. any actions taken to reduce and manage fraud risks;
f. any actions taken to ensure the proper management of investors' personal data and information, pursuant to Legislative Decree dated June 30, 2003 no. 196, and any modification thereafter;
g. any actions taken to manage conflicts of interest;
h. any actions taken to deal with complaints and the address to which complaints must be sent;
i. the mechanisms for the alternative dispute resolution;
j. the aggregate data concerning the offers made through the web platform and their results;
k. the relevant legislation, the indication of the hyperlink to the register, to the investor education section of the CONSOB website and to the special section of the Company Register provided by article 25, paragraph 8, of the decree;
l. details of any sanctions and precautionary provisions adopted by the CONSOB;
m. the actions that the web platform will take against issuers in the case of failure to observe the web platform functioning rules; the eventual lack of initiatives must be indicated as well.

Art. 15

(*Information about the investment in innovative start-ups*)

1. The web platform must provide investors with information about the investment in financial instruments of innovative start-ups, in a brief and easily comprehensible form, even by multimedia techniques; such information will include at least:

   a. the risk of losing the entire investment;
   b. the risk of illiquidity;
   c. the ban of dividend distribution under article 25 of the decree;
   d. the taxation of the investments (especially regarding the temporary nature of the tax benefits and their loss);
   e. the derogations either from corporate law under article 26 of the decree and from bankruptcy law under article 31 of the decree;
   f. the typical contents of a business plan;
   g. the withdrawal right pursuant to article 13, paragraph 5, and its exercise process.

2. The web platform must ensure that non-professional investors may access those sections of the web platform where it is possible to subscribe single offers, only if:

   a. they have undertaken investor education provided by article 14, paragraph 1, letter k) and the information referred to in paragraph 1;
   b. they have positively answered to a questionnaire giving evidence that they fully understood the essential features and main risks of on-line investment in innovative start-ups;
   c. they have declared that they can financially sustain the potential entire loss of the planned investment.

Art. 16

(*Information about the offers*)

1. For each offer, the web platform must publish:

a) the information indicated in Annex 3 and any updates thereof received from the issuer, also if significant changes occur or material mistakes are discovered during the offer, sharing each update with those who already subscribed the offer.

b) identification details of the banks or investment companies which process the orders and the identification details of the bank account referred to by article 17, paragraph 6;

c) details of the procedures for the exercise of the right of revocation referred to by article 25, paragraph 2;

d) the ways and frequency by which the information on the subscriptions, their amount and the number of subscribers will be provided.

2. The information indicated in paragraph 1 can also be provided by multimedia techniques. The web platform shall allow the acquisition on a hard driver of the information specified in paragraph 1, letter a).

Art. 17

(Obligations related to the processing of investment orders)

1. The web platform shall take actions to ensure that subscriptions received from the investors are:

a. quickly, correctly and efficiently processed;
b. promptly and accurately registered;
c. duly transmitted, together with each investor's identity details, following the chronological receipt sequence.

2. Banks and investment companies process the orders received from a web platform, keeping it informed of their outcomes, and ensuring fulfillment of what is stated under paragraph 6.

3. Banks and investment companies receiving orders shall behave with investors in compliance with the applicable provisions contained in Part II of the Consolidated Finance Act and any implementation rules thereafter.

4. The rules provided by paragraph 3 shall not apply in the following cases:

a) if the orders are issued by individuals and their consideration is less than five hundred euros per single order or one thousand euros for all the orders placed in a single year;

b) if the orders are issued by subjects different from individuals and their consideration is less than five thousand euros per single order or ten thousand euros for all the orders placed in a single year.

5. The web platform shall acquire from the investor a recordable statement declaring that, in the year of reference, the investor has not exceeded the threshold indicated in paragraph 4. For this purpose, the total amount shall include the investments processed either through the receiving web platform and any other web platforms.

6. The web platform must take care that, for each offer, the funds are deposited on an escrow account in the issuer's name at the banks and investment companies to which the orders are transmitted, pursuant to article 25.

Art. 18

**(*Obligations relating to investor protection from*

operational risks)

1. The web platform shall ensure the integrity of the information received and published by mean of reliable and secure operating systems.

2. In compliance with the requirement of paragraph 1, the web platform:

a) shall identify and manage the sources of operating risks, adopting adequate procedures and controls, also to avoid operational interruptions;

b) shall adopt appropriate back-up devices.

Art. 19

(*Confidentiality obligations*)

1. The web platform shall ensure the confidentiality of the information acquired from the investors in the business, except for the purposes connected with the processing of the offer by the issuer, as well as in any other case in which disclosure is required or allowed by law.

Art. 20

(*Record keeping obligation*)

1. The web platform shall neatly store for five years at least, in electronic or paper format, copies of the correspondence and the contractual documentation related to the web platform management, including:

- a. receipts of the subscriptions placed through the web platform and of the withdrawal and revocation rights exercised;
- b. transmissions of the orders to the banks and investment companies for the subscription of the

financial instruments offered;
c. receipts of the confirmations of the subscriptions of the financial instruments offered;
d. the certification set forth by article 17, paragraph 5.

Art. 21

(*Disclosure to CONSOB*)

1. The web platform shall send to CONSOB, without delay, any information about:

   a. amendments of the articles of association;
   b. any changes concerning the controlling shareholders, with indication of the respective shares in value and in percentage, together with the integrity requirements declaration pursuant to article 8;
   c. changes of administrators, directors and controllers, with their powers and any delegation, together with the integrity and professionalism declaration pursuant to article 9;
   d. any communications received pursuant to article 10, paragraph 1;
   e. any on suspension or revocation resolutions, adopted pursuant to article 11, paragraph 2.

2. The web platform shall communicate to CONSOB without delay the starting, interruption and resumption dates of business.

3. By March 31 each year, the web platform shall transmit to CONSOB:

   a. the report about the activities performed and the organizational structure according to the scheme provided by Annex 2, giving evidence to any changes occurred. In case of no changes, the report may be avoided, nevertheless such circumstance must be communicated;
   b. the data on web platform activities, showing at least the aggregate information about the

previous year offers and their results, as well as the ancillary services performed;
c. the data about service interruptions and their duration, together with the description of the actions taken to resume regular service;
d. the data about written complaints, remedies for deficiencies found and the activities planned.

Title IV

Sanctions and precautionary measures

Art. 22

(Precautionary measures)

1. In case of need and urgency, CONSOB may order a precautionary suspension of the operations of the web platform for a term no longer than ninety days, whenever there is valid ground for serious infringements of law or of general or specific provisions issued by CONSOB, pursuant to which the platform could be struck off the register.

Art. 23

(Sanctions)

1. Without prejudice to the provisions of article 50-*quinquies*, paragraph 7, first sentence, of the Consolidated Finance Act concerning fines, CONSOB shall order:

a) the suspension of the web platform operations in case of breach of the rules of conduct set forth by title III;

b) the cancellation from the register in the case of:

1) facilitating the collection of equity without the conditions established by article 24 or on behalf of companies other than innovative start-ups, including start-ups with social purposes, as defined by article 25, paragraphs 2 and 4 of the decree;

2) falsifying the investor's signature on the contractual forms or on other digital or analogue documentation;

3) keeping money third parties' financial instruments, even if temporarily;

4) communication or transmission of false or untrue information or documents to the investor or to CONSOB;

5) transmission to banks and investment companies of subscription orders for financial instruments not duly authorized by the investor;

6) failure to communicate to banks and investment companies that an investor has exercised the withdrawal right pursuant to article 13, section 5, or the revocation right pursuant to article 25;

7) repetition of behaviors that has given rise to a suspension order adopted pursuant to letter *a*);

8) every other breach of specific rules of conduct of particular severity.

PART III

RULES ABOUT OFFERS THROUGH WEB PLATFORMS

Art. 24

(Terms concerning the offers on the web platform)

1. Before admitting an offer on the web site, the web platform must check that under the issuer's articles of association or deed of incorporation:

a) would the controlling shareholders transfer the company's control to third parties after the offer, non-professional investors or investors other than those indicated in paragraph 2, which have purchased or subscribed financial instruments offered through a web platform, shall be granted a withdrawal right from the company or a tag along right, whose terms and conditions shall be stated. Such rights shall be granted for the whole time when the requirements set forth by article 25, paragraphs 2 and 4 of the decree are fulfilled and, in any case, for at least three years from the closing of the offer;

b) shareholders' agreements must be communicated to the company and published on the issuer's web site.

2. The effectiveness of the offer on the website is subject to the audit by the web platform that at least 5% of the financial instruments offered are subscribed by professional investors or by bank foundations or by innovative start-up incubators, pursuant to article 25, paragraph 5, of the decree.

Art. 25

(Funding and right of revocation)

1. The money for the subscriptions execution must be deposited on an escrow account in the name of the

issuer at the bank or investment company which received the orders. The account can not be credited before the date of subscription by the investor.

2. Non-professional investors who have given consent to subscribe financial instruments offered on an equity crowdfunding web platform have the right to revoke their consent when, between the subscription date and the definitive execution date, any new fact arises or a relevant clerical mistake occurs concerning the information provided on the web platform, which could affect the investment decision. The revocation right can be exercised within seven days from the date on which the new information is communicated to the investors.

3. Would the withdrawal or revocation right be exercised, or would the offer not be closed and executed, the funds referred to in paragraph 1 shall be fully returned to the investors.

ANNEX 1

INSTRUCTIONS FOR THE APPLICATION TO THE WEB PLATFORMS REGISTER AND FOR THE COMMUNICATION AT THE PURPOSE OF ANNOTATION IN THE SPECIAL SECTION

A. *Application for the registration*

1. The application for the registration, duly undersigned by the company's legal representative, shall specify the company name, the company's registered office and the administrative office, the address of the permanent establishment in the Italy for EU companies, the name and contact details of a company representative and the list of the annexed documents.

2. The application shall include the following documents:

a) copy of the deed of incorporation and of the articles of association together with a self-statement pursuant to Decree of the President of the Republic dated December 28, 2000 no. 445, substituting the Company Register certification of the current legal existence of the company;

b) the list of controlling shareholders with indication of their respective shares in value and in percentage, with indication of the nominee for indirect shareholdings;

c) the documentation to check the reputation requirements of the controlling shareholders;

i) *for individuals*:

— self-statement or certification (pursuant to articles 46 and 47 of the Decree of the President of the Republic dated December 28, 2000 no. 445) certifying the lack of any situation set forth by article 8 of the Regulation;

— self-statement pursuant to articles 46 of the Decree of the President of the Republic dated December 28, 2000 no. 445, about the "anti-mafia" Company Register certification.

ii) *for corporate entities*:

— minutes of meeting of the board of directors or equivalent body giving evidence of the verification of the requirements held by the directors and the general manager, or by those holding performing equivalent duties in the controlling company or entity;

d) list of the names of all the administrators, directors and controllers;

e) minutes of the meeting in which the management body has verified the reputation and professionalism requirements for each administrator, director and controller, together with the annexes thereof;

f) a report on the company business and organizational structure drafted according to Annex 2.

B. *Communication for annotation in the special section of the register*

1. Before starting operations, banks and investment companies, authorized to perform investment services,

shall communicate their equity crowdfunding web platform service, indicating the company name, the web site URL, its hyperlink, the name and contact details of a company representative. The company's legal representative shall undersign the communication.

ANNEX 2

REPORT ON THE COMPANY'S BUSINESS AND ORGANIZATIONAL STRUCTURE

A. *Company business*

The web platform must describe in detail the activity it intends to perform. In particular, the following must be indicated:

1. the methods adopted to select the offers to display on the web site;
2. any advisory service provided to the innovative start-ups concerning strategic analyses and financial assessments, business strategy and related matters;
3. whether periodic information will be published about any reached milestones and/or periodic reports on the trend of the innovative start-up whose financial instruments have been offered on the web platform;
4. whether any mechanisms will be implemented for the periodic evaluation of the financial instruments subscribed or for price monitoring in the following transactions;

5. whether any mechanisms will be implemented to facilitate information flows between the innovative start-up and its investors, or among investors;
6. any other activities.

B. *Organizational structure*

The web platform shall provide at least the following information:

1. a description of the company structure (organizational chart, chart of offices, etc.) explaining any delegated powers, any control mechanisms implemented and any other useful element to illustrate the web platform's operational features;
2. the recruiting plan, if any, and the relative implementation stage, or indication of the current employees that will be involved in the business. The plan shall mention the availability of any employees or collaborators who have carried out professional or academic or certified research activities at public or private universities and/or research institutes in Italy or abroad, about matters concerning corporate finance and/or business economics and/or corporate law and/or marketing and/or new technologies and/or technical-scientific matters, with indication of the roles and functions performed within the company organization;
3. any procedures, including the digital ones, to ensure the fulfillment of the obligations set forth in articles 13, 14, 15 and 16 of this regulation;
4. any systems for processing the orders received from the investors and in particular to ensure the compliance with the terms provided by article 17, paragraph 2, of this regulation;
5. the procedures for the transmission of the investors orders to banks and investment

companies;
6. description of the digital infrastructure developed for receiving and transmitting the investors orders (reliability, security, integrity, privacy, etc.);
7. place and methods for documentation storage;
8. conflicts of interest identification and management policy;
9. fraud prevention and privacy protection policy;
10. any outsourcing:
    a) of the strategy for the selection of the offers to be presented on the web platform, with specification of the scope and content of the mandate;
    b) of any other activities or services.
    In particular, the activities outsourced, subjects mandated, contents of the mandates and measures to ensure control on outsourced activities and to mitigate the risks involved must be specified;
11. any existence of mandates for the selection of the offers received by other web platform, indicating their scope and contents;
12. the fee structure for the services offered by the web platform.

This Annex is part of the provisions adopted under article 50-*quinquies*, paragraph 5, letter *a*) of the Consolidated Finance Act and it also aims to contribute to the information base (to be periodically updated) available to CONSOB and which can help to direct and schedule the monitoring action.

ANNEX 3

INFORMATION ABOUT THE OFFER

1. Warning

The web platform must ensure that for each offer the following warning, graphically highlighted, is preliminary displayed: "The information on the offer is not subjected to approval by CONSOB. The issuer is the sole subject responsible for the completeness and truth of the data and information supplied by the same. The investor must also take note of the fact that an investment in financial instruments issued by innovative start-ups cannot necessarily be cashed in and features a very high risk.

2. Information about risks

Description of the specific risks concerning the issuer and of the offer.

3. Information about the issuer and the financial instruments offered

a. description of the issuer, of the business project with indication of the social sector of activity in the case of an innovative start-up having social purposes, of their business plan and indication of the hyperlinks to the issuer's website where the information required by article 25, paragraphs 11 and 12, of the decree can be found;
b. description of the corporate bodies and the track record of the company directors;
c. description of the financial instruments offered, and of any inherent rights including exercise terms and conditions;
d. description of the clauses set by the issuer for the cases in which the controlling shareholders sell their own shares to third parties after the offer (investment way-out procedures, the existence of any repurchase agreements, lock-up and put option clauses in favor of the investors, etc.) including their duration, according to article 24.

4. **Information about the offer**

a. general terms and conditions of the offer, including addressees, and any clauses governing the effectiveness and the possibility of revocation;
b. information about any shareholding already subscribed by professional investors or by the other investors listed under article 24, including their identity;
c. indication of any costs or commissions charged to the investor, including any expenses for the order transmission to banks and investment companies;
d. description of the methods for calculating the stake reserved to professional investors or the other categories of investors listed under article 24, and procedures and terms for the publication of the update on the state of the subscriptions;

e. indication of the banks and investment companies to which the subscription orders will be transmitted and the description of the inherent procedure and timing, as well as any existence of conflicts of interest involving such banks and investment companies;
f. information about the escrow account opened pursuant to article 17, paragraph 6, and on the date of the effective debit of funds in the subscribers accounts;
g. information about the refund procedures, would withdrawal or revocation rights be duly exercised, or would subscription not be duly completed;
h. terms and conditions for the payment and the delivery of the financial instruments subscribed;
i. information about any conflicts of interest involved with the offer, including those arising from agreements between the issuer and the web platform, their controlling shareholders, administrators, directors, controllers, professional investors or other investors listed under article 24 which have already subscribed the reserved shares;
j. information about concurrent offers of the same financial instruments on other web platforms;
k. the applicable law and the jurisdiction;
l. the language or languages in which the information on the offer is provided.

5. Information about any services offered by the web platform in relation to the offer

Description of the activities connected to the offer performed by the web platform.

* * *

[Certain qualitative requirements of the offer form are also defined]

The information about the offer shall be easily understandable to a reasonable investor and must be given in a non-technical language, without specific jargon; it shall be clear and concise, and shall make use of plain language. The information shall also be comparable with the other offers of the web platform.

Presentation and structure of the document shall facilitate the reading by the investors, also as far as the fonts size is concerned. The document must be no longer than five A4 pages. If company colors or logos are used, they must not compromise the understanding of the information, if the document is printed or copied in black and white.

www.ingramcontent.com/pod-product-compliance
Lightning Source LLC
Chambersburg PA
CBHW071802200526
45167CB00017B/1174